REACT.JS: EASY LEARNING

SANDEEP BISHT

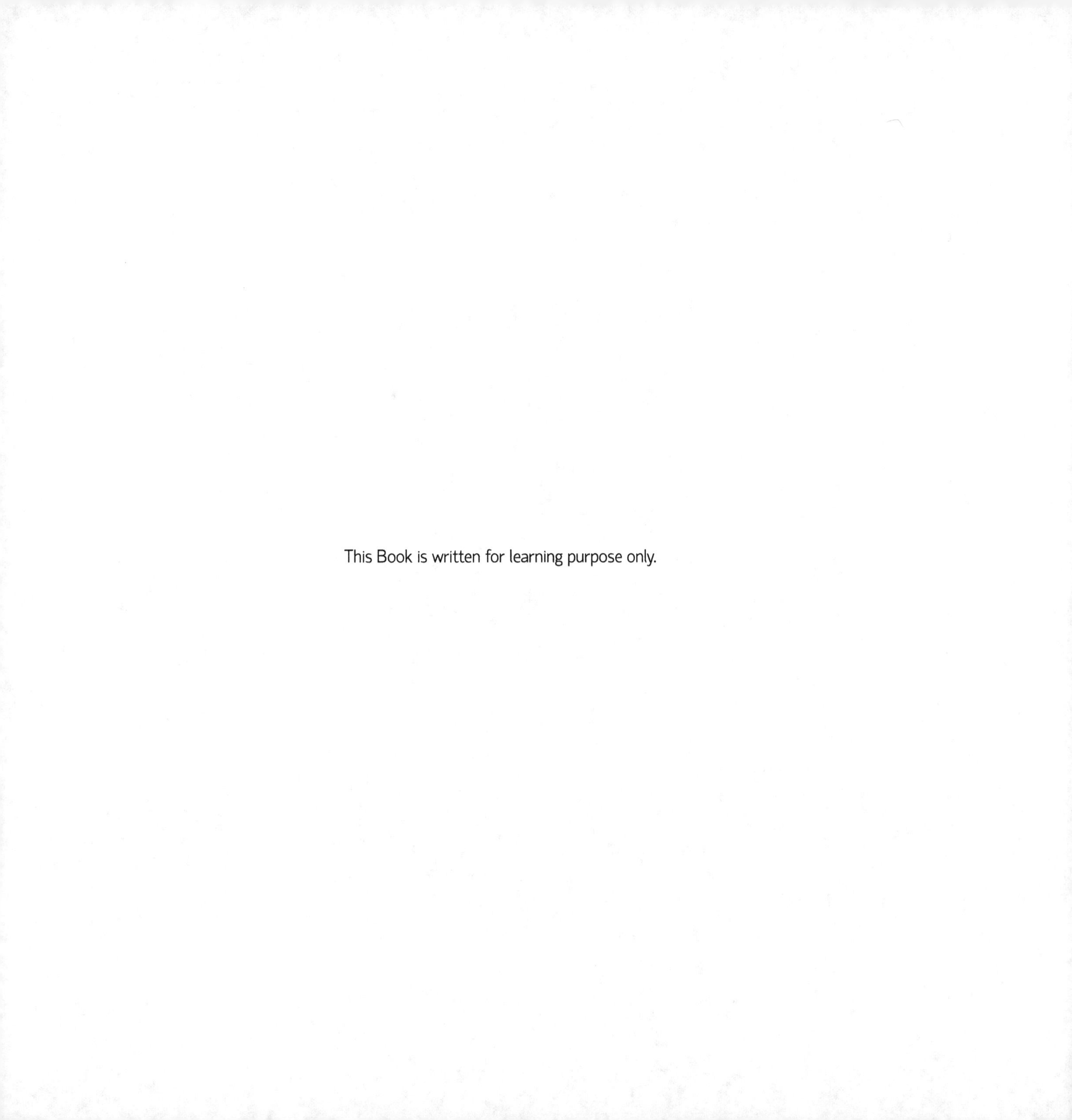

This Book is written for learning purpose only.

Contents

Foreword

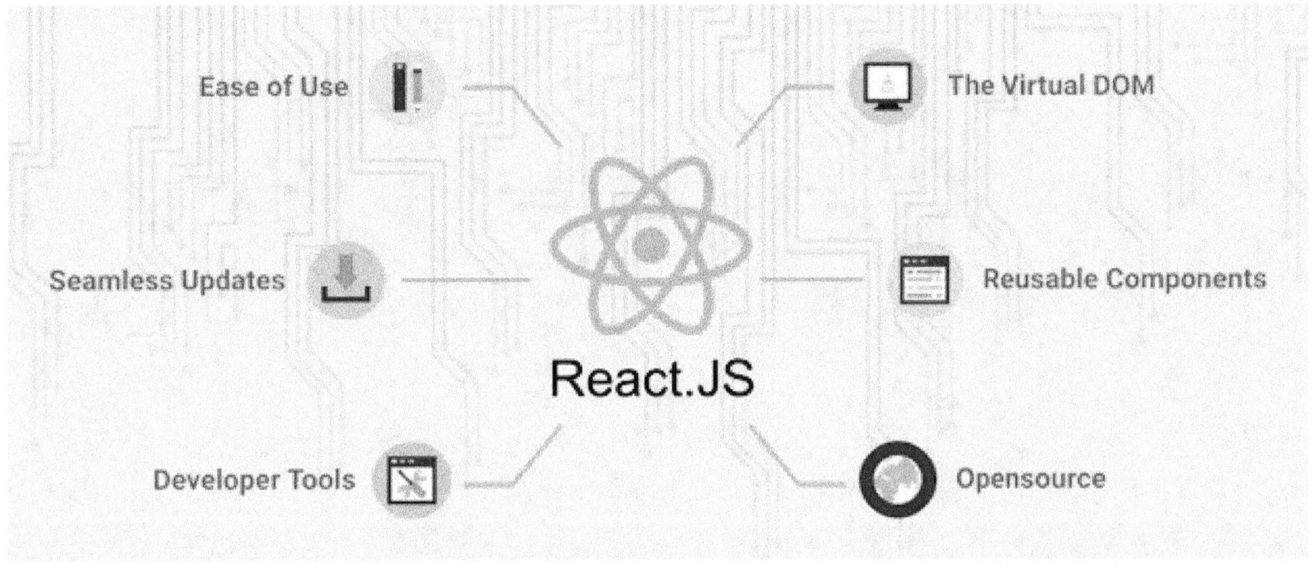

React.js Library

Preface

I realize that this book will create a great deal of UI development in React.js. It has never been easy to challenge the consensus because the System – of any kind, in any context – will try to preserve the status quo, by all means possible. Having spent 7 years in the field of frontend-development, backend-development and deployment, and having published lots of papers, including 7 reviews and book chapters on different aspects of developments, I feel obliged to share my knowledge, analyses, and conclusions. Hopefully, this account will raise the level of awareness among the general public and initiate the discussion that, in turn, may entail major cultural changes, as well as a revision of the consumer basket. The beneficiaries will be all of us – ourselves, our children, our beloved ones, the society, as a whole – who will want to live with new technology, and longer, life.

Acknowledgements

CHAPTER ONE

React.js

Q: What is React?

Ans*: React is a JavaScript library for creating user interfaces by Facebook and Instagram.*

https://reactjs.org/tutorial/tutorial.html

Q: What problem is React trying to solve?

Ans: "Building large applications with data that changes over time."

CHAPTER TWO

Hello World

I will walk you through how a simple component is built.

```
var HelloMessage = React.createClass({
  displayName: 'HelloMessage',
  render: function() {
    return React.DOM.div(null, "Hello ", this.props.name);
  }
});
```

This the code for the HelloMessage component.

```
var HelloMessage = React.createClass({
  displayName: 'HelloMessage',
  render: function() {
    return React.DOM.div(null, "Hello ", this.props.name);
  }
});
```

This call creates a React component. FYI, createClass might be a bit misleading because as you'll later see, React components are not instantiated with the new keyword and are actually more like a function in the mathematical sense: They take input and generate one output, in this case a DOM tree.

```
var HelloMessage = React.createClass({
  displayName: 'HelloMessage',
  render: function() {
    return React.DOM.div(null, "Hello ", this.props.name);
  }
});
```

It's best practice to give your component a displayName. This is only used during debugging, when the displayName will be used to tell you where a problem occurred.

```
var HelloMessage = React.createClass({
  displayName: 'HelloMessage',
  render: function() {
    return React.DOM.div(null, "Hello ", this.props.name);
  }
});
```

React components only have to expose one function which is render.

```
var HelloMessage = React.createClass({
  displayName: 'HelloMessage',
  render: function() {
    return React.DOM.div(null, "Hello ", this.props.name);
  }
});
```

render is a function that should return the DOM representation of your component at any point in time.

```
var HelloMessage = React.createClass({
  displayName: 'HelloMessage',
  render: function() {
    return React.DOM.div(null, "Hello ", this.props.name);
  }
});
```

In this case we'll return a
element, which lives in the React.DOM namespace.

```
var HelloMessage = React.createClass({
  displayName: 'HelloMessage',
  render: function() {
    return React.DOM.div(null, "Hello ", this.props.name);
  }
});
         {id: 'message', className: 'hidden'}
```

The first argument is where you can add element attributes such as ID or class name, in this case we simply omit them using null

```
var HelloMessage = React.createClass({
  displayName: 'HelloMessage',
  render: function() {
    return React.DOM.div(null, "Hello ", this.props.name);
  }
});
```

The remaining arguments are the children of that component, in this case a simple string "Hello " and the property name.

```
var HelloMessage = React.createClass({
  displayName: 'HelloMessage',
  render: function() {
    return React.DOM.div(null, "Hello ", this.props.name);
  }
});
```

```
React.renderComponent(
  HelloMessage({name: "FiftyThree"}),
  mountNode
);
```

```
<div data-reactid=".dbuc1iytj4" data-react-checksum="-695455966">
  <span data-reactid=".dbuc1iytj4.0">Hello </span>
  <span data-reactid=".dbuc1iytj4.1">FiftyThree</span>
</div>
```

Let's look at how a component is rendered...

```
var HelloMessage = React.createClass({
  displayName: 'HelloMessage',
  render: function() {
    return React.DOM.div(null, "Hello ", this.props.name);
  }
});
```

```
React.renderComponent(
  HelloMessage({name: "FiftyThree"}),
  mountNode
);
```

```
<div data-reactid=".dbuc1iytj4" data-react-checksum="-695455966">
  <span data-reactid=".dbuc1iytj4.0">Hello </span>
  <span data-reactid=".dbuc1iytj4.1">FiftyThree</span>
</div>
```

React provides several rendering functions. The main one is renderComponent which renders a component into the browser DOM. It takes two arguments...

```
var HelloMessage = React.createClass({
  displayName: 'HelloMessage',
  render: function() {
    return React.DOM.div(null, "Hello ", this.props.name);
  }
});
```

```
React.renderComponent(
  HelloMessage({name: "FiftyThree"}),
  mountNode
);
```

```
<div data-reactid=".dbuc1iytj4" data-react-checksum="-695455966">
  <span data-reactid=".dbuc1iytj4.0">Hello </span>
  <span data-reactid=".dbuc1iytj4.1">FiftyThree</span>
</div>
```

...the first is a reference to the component itself...

```
var HelloMessage = React.createClass({
  displayName: 'HelloMessage',
  render: function() {
    return React.DOM.div(null, "Hello ", this.props.name);
  }
});
```

```
React.renderComponent(
  HelloMessage({name: "FiftyThree"}),
  mountNode /* e.g. `document.body` */
);
```

```
<div data-reactid=".dbuc1iytj4" data-react-checksum="-695455966">
  <span data-reactid=".dbuc1iytj4.0">Hello </span>
  <span data-reactid=".dbuc1iytj4.1">FiftyThree</span>
</div>
```

...and the second is which DOM node to mount into or to render into. For example, we could render directly into the body using document.body.

```
var HelloMessage = React.createClass({
  displayName: 'HelloMessage',
  render: function() {
    return React.DOM.div(null, "Hello ", this.props.name);
  }
});
```

```
React.renderComponent(
  HelloMessage({name: "FiftyThree"}),
  mountNode
);
```

```
<div data-reactid=".dbuc1iytj4" data-react-checksum="-695455966">
  <span data-reactid=".dbuc1iytj4.0">Hello </span>
  <span data-reactid=".dbuc1iytj4.1">FiftyThree</span>
</div>
```

Now you can also see how the result of render is reflected in the browser, in this case the div element. It's a one-to-one mapping of React DOM components to actual DOM elements. For now, please ignore the data-reactid and data-react-checksum attributes. I'll explain later what they are used for

```
var HelloMessage = React.createClass({
  displayName: 'HelloMessage',
  render: function() {
    return React.DOM.div(null, "Hello ", this.props.name);
  }
});
```

```
React.renderComponent(
  HelloMessage({name: "FiftyThree"}),
  mountNode
);
```

```
<div data-reactid=".dbuc1iytj4" data-react-checksum="-695455966">
  <span data-reactid=".dbuc1iytj4.0">Hello </span>
  <span data-reactid=".dbuc1iytj4.1">FiftyThree</span>
</div>
```

The dynamic properties are passed into the React component during rendering and are reflected in the browser.

```
var HelloMessage = React.createClass({
  displayName: 'HelloMessage',
  render: function() {
    return React.DOM.div(null, "Hello ", this.props.name);
  }
});
```

```
React.renderComponent(
  HelloMessage({name: "FiftyThree"}),
  mountNode
);
```

```
<div data-reactid=".dbuc1iytj4" data-react-checksum="-695455966">
  <span data-reactid=".dbuc1iytj4.0">Hello </span>
  <span data-reactid=".dbuc1iytj4.1">FiftyThree</span>
</div>
```

Hmm, if you've worked with other frameworks and toolkits before, you will probably feel that this is harder to read than regular HTML templates.

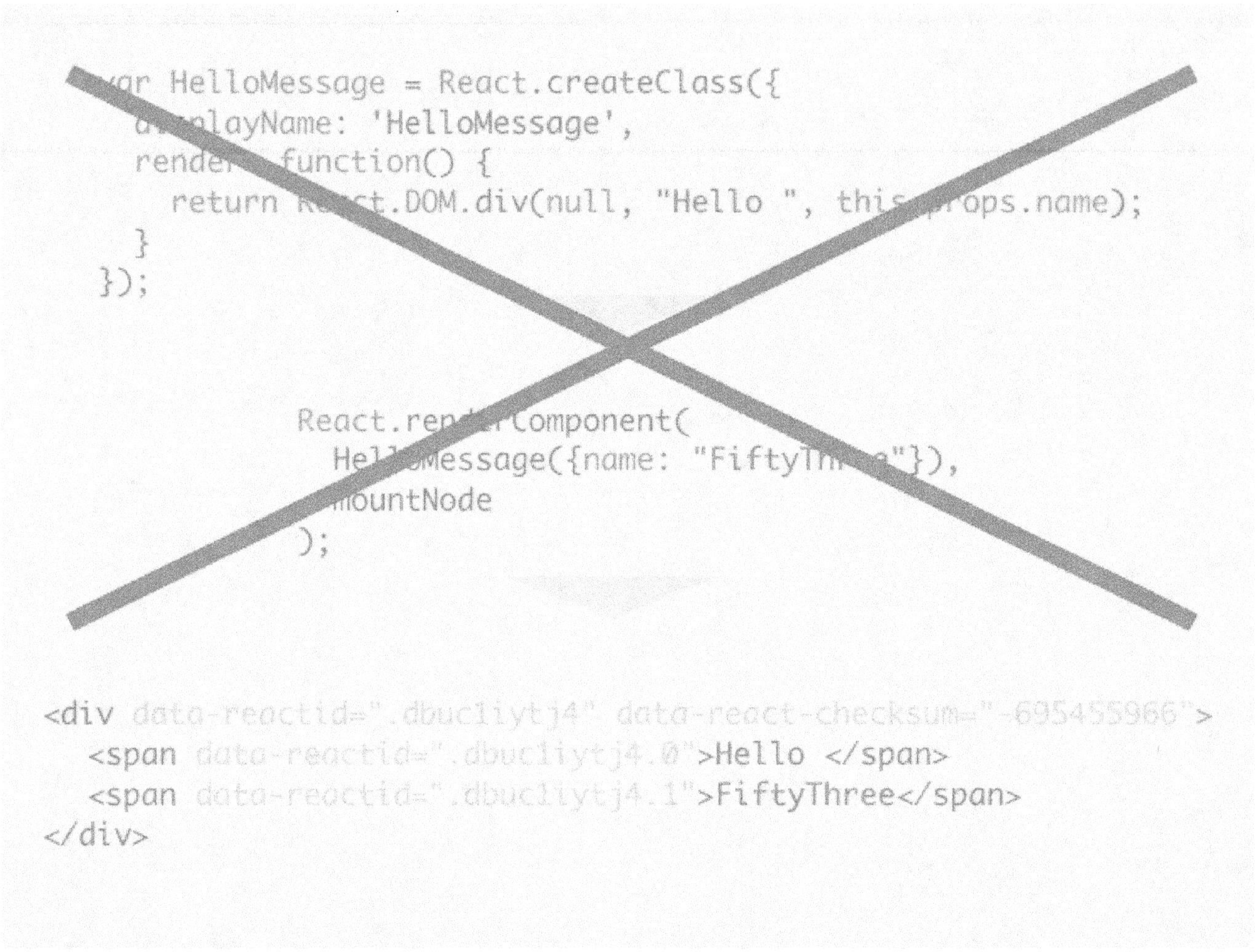

```
var HelloMessage = React.createClass({
  displayName: 'HelloMessage',
  render: function() {
    return React.DOM.div(null, "Hello ", this.props.name);
  }
});
```

```
React.renderComponent(
  HelloMessage({name: "FiftyThree"}),
  mountNode
);
```

```
<div data-reactid=".dbuc1iytj4" data-react-checksum="-695455966">
  <span data-reactid=".dbuc1iytj4.0">Hello </span>
  <span data-reactid=".dbuc1iytj4.1">FiftyThree</span>
</div>
```

You're not alone thinking that. The designers of React thought the same and that's why they created an alternate syntax for React components.

```
/** @jsx React.DOM */
var HelloMessage = React.createClass({
  render: function() {
    return <div>Hello {this.props.name}</div>;
  }
});
```

```
var HelloMessage = React.createClass({
  displayName: 'HelloMessage',
  render: function() {
    return React.DOM.div(null, "Hello ", this.props.name);
  }
});
```

```
React.renderComponent(
  <HelloMessage name="FiftyThree" />,
  mountNode
);
```

```
<div data-reactid=".dbuc1iytj4" data-react-checksum="-695455966">
   <span data-reactid=".dbuc1iytj4.0">Hello </span>
   <span data-reactid=".dbuc1iytj4.1">FiftyThree</span>
</div>
```

It's called JSX and is an XML-like syntax for creating React components. It is inspired by the now abandoned E4X standard for those of you who remember the ECMAScript 4 spec or have worked with ActionScript 3. Let's look at it a bit more closely

```
/** @jsx React.DOM */
var HelloMessage = React.createClass({
  render: function() {
    return <div>Hello {this.props.name}</div>;
  }
});

var HelloMessage = React.createClass({
  displayName: 'HelloMessage',
  render: function() {
    return React.DOM.div(null, "Hello ", this.props.name);
  }
});

React.renderComponent(
  <HelloMessage name="FiftyThree" />,
  mountNode
);

<div data-reactid=".dbuc1iytj4" data-react-checksum="-695455966">
  <span data-reactid=".dbuc1iytj4.0">Hello </span>
  <span data-reactid=".dbuc1iytj4.1">FiftyThree</span>
</div>
```

You write your components as usual but instead of calls to React.DOM.* you simply write HTML tags as you would in a template. The @jsx directive at the top tells the JSX compiler where to look up components, in this case div is looked up in React.DOM.

```
/** @jsx React.DOM */
var HelloMessage = React.createClass({
  render: function() {
    return <div>Hello {this.props.name}</div>;
  }
});
```

```
var HelloMessage = React.createClass({
  displayName: 'HelloMessage',
  render: function() {
    return React.DOM.div(null, "Hello ", this.props.name);
  }
});
```

```
React.renderComponent(
  <HelloMessage name="FiftyThree" />,
  mountNode
);
```

```
<div data-reactid=".dbuc1iytj4" data-react-checksum="-695455966">
   <span data-reactid=".dbuc1iytj4.0">Hello </span>
   <span data-reactid=".dbuc1iytj4.1">FiftyThree</span>
</div>
```

The same way you can use JSX inside your components, you can also use it to render your own components.

```
/** @jsx React.DOM */
var HelloMessage = React.createClass({
  render: function() {
    return <div>Hello {this.props.name}</div>;
  }
});
```

```
var HelloMessage = React.createClass({
  displayName: 'HelloMessage',
  render: function() {
    return React.DOM.div(null, "Hello ", this.props.name);
  }
});
```

```
React.renderComponent(
  <HelloMessage name="FiftyThree" />,
  mountNode
);
```

```
<div data-reactid=".dbuc1iytj4" data-react-checksum="-695455966">
  <span data-reactid=".dbuc1iytj4.0">Hello </span>
  <span data-reactid=".dbuc1iytj4.1">FiftyThree</span>
</div>
```

JSX has a special syntax for declaring and using dynamic properties, in this case name.

```
/** @jsx React.DOM */
var HelloMessage = React.createClass({
  render: function() {
    return <div>Hello {this.props.name}</div>;
  }
});


var HelloMessage = React.createClass({
  displayName: 'HelloMessage',
  render: function() {
    return React.DOM.div(null, "Hello ", this.props.name);
  }
});


     React.renderComponent(
       <HelloMessage name="FiftyThree" />,
       mountNode
     );


<div data-reactid=".dbucliytj4" data-react-checksum="-695455966">
   <span data-reactid=".dbucliytj4.0">Hello </span>
   <span data-reactid=".dbucliytj4.1">FiftyThree</span>
</div>
```

Unfortunately, this is not very helpful for those of us who found bliss in CoffeeScript as there is no JSX equivalent for CoffeeScript.

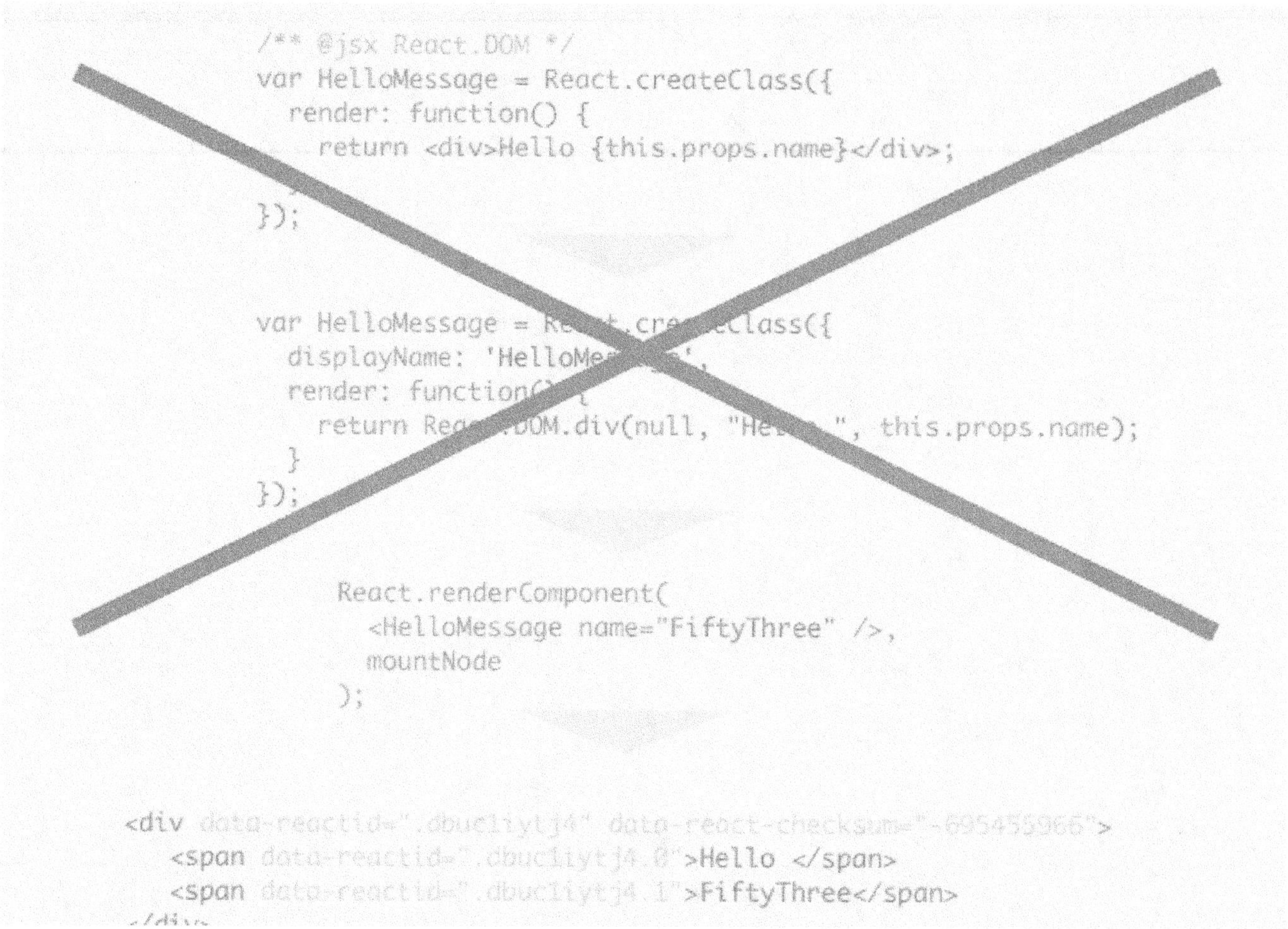

```
/** @jsx React.DOM */
var HelloMessage = React.createClass({
  render: function() {
    return <div>Hello {this.props.name}</div>;
  }
});
```

```
var HelloMessage = React.createClass({
  displayName: 'HelloMessage',
  render: function() {
    return React.DOM.div(null, "Hello ", this.props.name);
  }
});
```

```
React.renderComponent(
  <HelloMessage name="FiftyThree" />,
  mountNode
);
```

```
<div data-reactid=".dbuc1iytj4" data-react-checksum="-695455966">
  <span data-reactid=".dbuc1iytj4.0">Hello </span>
  <span data-reactid=".dbuc1iytj4.1">FiftyThree</span>
</div>
```

The good news is that it doesn't matter because...

CHAPTER THREE

Behind the Scenes

Let's have a look at what actually happens behind the scenes.

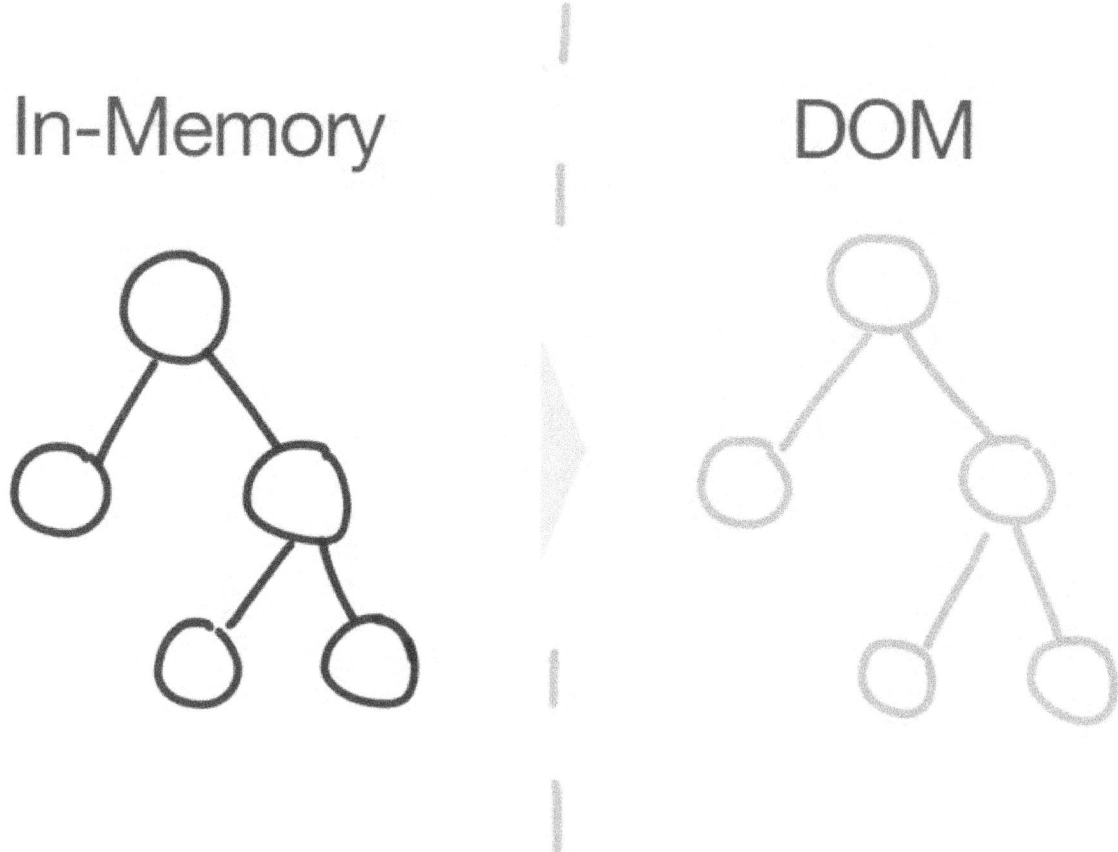

When React calls your component's render function, it uses its return value to construct an in-memory representation of the DOM. Then this virtual DOM is rendered from memory into the actual DOM. On the initial render, this is not very different from regular template rendering, except we're dealing with objects and trees in memory instead of just a string.

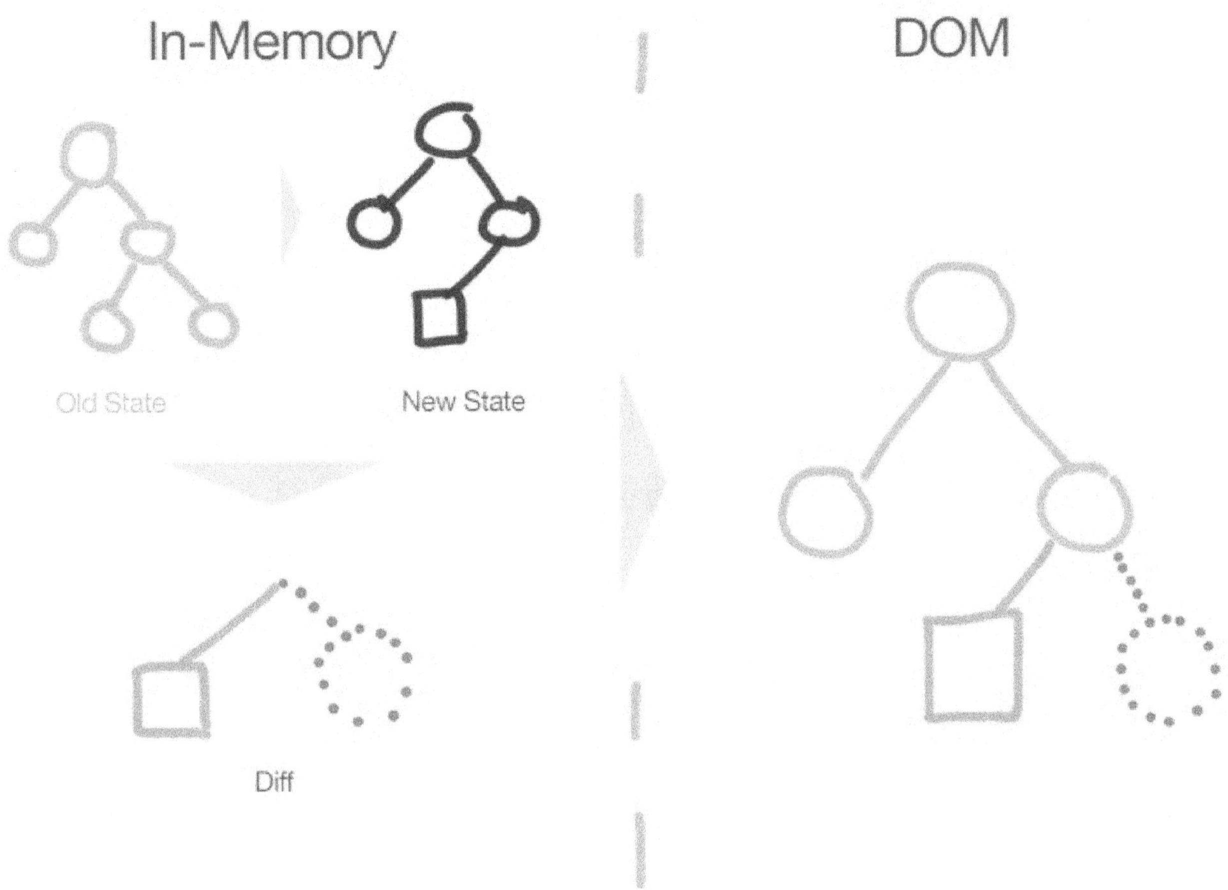

Where it gets interesting is when we have subsequent updates, for example when you call setState or when you call renderComponent again, React creates a new virtual representation of the DOM based on the current inputs (props and state) as seen in tree marked New State in the left panel. In this case, we changed the left leaf of the right node (square box) and removed the other leaf. Since React didn't actually throw away the previous representation of the DOM (Old State), it can run an efficient diff of the the two trees in memory, which is far faster than accessing the real DOM. Once the minimal set of changes in your virtual DOM are identified (based on heuristics), they are applied to the actual DOM as a batch. This leaves us with the latest state of our app in the browser.

http://facebook.github.io/react/docs/reconciliation.html

CHAPTER FOUR

Benefits

Let's look at benefits of this rendering mechanism.

* **Simple**: It's simple because from a developer's point of view, you simply trigger a re-render of your app on every update just like you would in a server-rendered app. React makes sure the changes are applied correctly...

* **Fast**: ...and efficiently. React is fast because operations happen in-memory without accessing the actual DOM which is usually the major performance bottleneck.

* **Synthetic events**: Because React has a virtual DOM, it also implements synthetic events. They look, smell and feel like real events, except that they behave the same across all browsers that React supports. In case you need to, you can still access the native event using event.nativeEvent.

CHAPTER FIVE

Goodies

Let me present some goodness I found in React and its add-ons.

* PropTypes: PropTypes let us validate input properties.

```
React.createClass
  displayName: 'Avatar'

  propTypes:
    # Required
    user: React.PropTypes.object.isRequired

    # Optional
    includeLink: React.PropTypes.bool
    size: React.PropTypes.oneOf ['micro', 'small',
      'medium', 'large']



        Avatar
          includeLink: 'http://gasi.ch/'
          size: 'medium'
```

Looking at a simple Avatar component...

```
React.createClass
  displayName: 'Avatar'

  propTypes:
    # Required
    user: React.PropTypes.object.isRequired

    # Optional
    includeLink: React.PropTypes.bool
    size: React.PropTypes.oneOf ['micro', 'small',
      'medium', 'large']


          Avatar
            includeLink: 'http://gasi.ch/'
            size: 'medium'
```

...we can define propTypes which will check properties we pass into the component when it is created.

```
React.createClass
  displayName: 'Avatar'

  propTypes:
    # Required
    user: React.PropTypes.object.isRequired

    # Optional
    includeLink: React.PropTypes.bool
    size: React.PropTypes.oneOf ['micro', 'small',
      'medium', 'large']
```

```
Avatar
  includeLink: 'http://gasi.ch/'
  size: 'medium'
```

Required properties can be defined by adding isRequired to the property definition. Here we require user to be of type object and always be present. In this case, React would give us a warning during development because we didn't include it.

```
React.createClass
  displayName: 'Avatar'

  propTypes:
    # Required
    user: React.PropTypes.object.isRequired

    # Optional
    includeLink: React.PropTypes.bool
    size: React.PropTypes.oneOf ['micro', 'small',
      'medium', 'large']

            Avatar
              includeLink: 'http://gasi.ch/'
              size: 'medium'
```

Optional properties are simply defined without isRequired.

```
React.createClass
  displayName: 'Avatar'

  propTypes:
    # Required
    user: React.PropTypes.object.isRequired

    # Optional
    includeLink: React.PropTypes.bool
    size: React.PropTypes.oneOf ['micro', 'small',
      'medium', 'large']
```

```
Avatar
  includeLink: 'http://gasi.ch/'
  size: 'medium'
```

size passes validation because it corresponds to one of the predefined values.

CHAPTER SIX

Server-Side Rendering

...or how to (hopefully) make your initial page loads faster and your Google ranking go up.

```
app.get '/', (req, res) ->
    props =
        currentUser:
            firstName: 'Sandeep'
            lastName: 'Bisht'
    content = React.renderComponentToString App props
    res.render 'app.toffee', {content, props}
```

```
<!doctype html>
<html>
<body>
    #{raw content}
    <script src="http://fb.me/react-0.10.0.js"></script>
    <script src="/scripts/app.js"></script>
    <script>
        React.renderComponent(App(#{props}), document.body);
    </script>
</body>
</html>
```

Once you write your app in React, turning on server-side rendering is fairly straightforward.

```
app.get '/', (req, res) ->
    props =
        currentUser:
            firstName: 'Sandeep'
            lastName: 'Bisht'
    content = React.renderComponentToString App props
    res.render 'app.toffee', {content, props}
```

```
<!doctype html>
<html>
<body>
    #{raw content}
    <script src="http://fb.me/react-0.10.0.js"></script>
    <script src="/scripts/app.js"></script>
    <script>
        React.renderComponent(App(#{props}), document.body);
    </script>
</body>
</html>
```

You take your props and create your app top-level component...

```
app.get '/', (req, res) ->
    props =
        currentUser:
            firstName: 'Sandeep'
            lastName: 'Bisht'
    content = React.renderComponentToString App props
    res.render 'app.toffee', {content, props}
```

```
<!doctype html>
<html>
<body>
    #{raw content}
    <script src="http://fb.me/react-0.10.0.js"></script>
    <script src="/scripts/app.js"></script>
    <script>
        React.renderComponent(App(#{props}), document.body);
    </script>
</body>
</html>
```

...then you use one React's alternative rendering functions—renderComponentToString—to create a string representation of the DOM.

```
app.get '/', (req, res) ->
    props =
        currentUser:
            firstName: 'Sandeep'
            lastName: 'Bisht'
    content = React.renderComponentToString App props
    res.render 'app.toffee', {content, props}
```

```
<!doctype html>
<html>
<body>
    #{raw content}
    <script src="http://fb.me/react-0.10.0.js"></script>
    <script src="/scripts/app.js"></script>
    <script>
        React.renderComponent(App(#{props}), document.body);
    </script>
</body>
</html>
```

Next you render your HTML and properties into your server-side template.

```
app.get '/', (req, res) ->
    props =
        currentUser:
            firstName: 'Sandeep'
            lastName: 'Bisht'
    content = React.renderComponentToString App props
    res.render 'app.toffee', {content, props}


<!doctype html>
<html>
<body>
    #{raw content}
    <script src="http://fb.me/react-0.10.0.js"></script>
    <script src="/scripts/app.js"></script>
    <script>
        React.renderComponent(App(#{props}), document.body);
    </script>
</body>
</html>
```

Include React.js

```
  app.get '/', (req, res) ->
      props =
          currentUser:
              firstName: 'Sandeep'
              lastName: 'Bisht'
      content = React.renderComponentToString App props
      res.render 'app.toffee', {content, props}
```

```
<!doctype html>
<html>
<body>
    #{raw content}
    <script src="http://fb.me/react-0.10.0.js"></script>
    <script src="/scripts/app.js"></script>
    <script>
        React.renderComponent(App(#{props}), document.body);
    </script>
</body>
</html>
```

Include your app script.

```
app.get '/', (req, res) ->
    props =
        currentUser:
            firstName: 'Sandeep'
            lastName: 'Bisht'
    content = React.renderComponentToString App props
    res.render 'app.toffee', {content, props}
```

```
<!doctype html>
<html>
<body>
    #{raw content}
    <script src="http://fb.me/react-0.10.0.js"></script>
    <script src="/scripts/app.js"></script>
    <script>
        React.renderComponent(App(#{props}), document.body);
    </script>
</body>
</html>
```

Finally, we make a client-side React render call, using the renderComponent. This is were the magic happens.

```
<div data-reactid=".dbuc1iytj4" data-react-checksum="-695455966">
  <span data-reactid=".dbuc1iytj4.0">Hello </span>
  <span data-reactid=".dbuc1iytj4.1">FiftyThree</span>
</div>
```

Remember that first HTML snippet that React generated for us in the HelloMessage component? Back then I asked you to ignore the data-reactid and data-react-checksum attributes.

```
<div data-reactid=".dbuc1iytj4" data-react-checksum="-695455966">
  <span data-reactid=".dbuc1iytj4.0">Hello </span>
  <span data-reactid=".dbuc1iytj4.1">FiftyThree</span>
</div>
```

I'd like to now explain what they're good for. The data-reactid attribute is for React to look up the child components of your app and register the clientside event handlers that the server simply ignores.

```
<div data-reactid=".dbuc1iytj4" data-react-checksum="-695455966">
  <span data-reactid=".dbuc1iytj4.0">Hello </span>
  <span data-reactid=".dbuc1iytj4.1">FiftyThree</span>
</div>
```

The data-react-checksum attribute is used to verify that the HTML the server generated is valid on the client-side. You might ask yourself, how could it be invalid? I originally asked myself the same thing but then ran into a quirky case. The component was working with was Retina aware and rendered certain images in the UI with higher resolution if the client had a high DPI screen. We used window.devicePixelRatio on the client-side but when this rendered on the server, it evaluated to undefined and the fallback was the value 1 which means the UI was rendered assuming the client didn't have a high DPI screen. Turns out, when the user does have a high DPI screen, React re-

renders the entire component and notices the checksum doesn't match because window.devicePixelRatio is 2 and not 1, so the server-side render was wasted. A workaround to this problem would be to use heuristics based on user agent and other factors to determine if the client has a high DPI screen.

CHAPTER SEVEN

CSSTransitionGroup

How to animate stuff in React.

Component

```
render: ->
  React.addons.CSSTransitionGroup
    transitionName: 'notification'
  ,
    if @state.notification
      Notification {message: @state.notification}
    else
      []
```

Enter Styles

```
.notification
  &-enter
    opacity: 0.01
    transition: opacity 0.2s ease-in

    &-active
      opacity: 1
```

Leave Styles

```
.notification
  &-leave
    opacity: 1
    transition: opacity 0.1s ease-in

    &-active
      opacity: 0.01
```

Imagine a simple notification component that fades in when there is a new notification and quickly fades out when the notification disappears.

Stylus: http://learnboost.github.io/stylus/

Component

```
render: ->
  React.addons.CSSTransitionGroup
    transitionName: 'notification'
  ,
    if @state.notification
      Notification {message: @state.notification}
    else
      []
```

Enter Styles*

```
.notification
  &-enter
    opacity: 0.01
    transition: opacity 0.2s ease-in

    &-active
      opacity: 1
```

Leave Styles*

```
.notification
  &-leave
    opacity: 1
    transition: opacity 0.1s ease-in

    &-active
      opacity: 0.01
```

Inside the render function, we wrap our component in CSSTransitionGroup that is provided as a React add-on. http://facebook.github.io/react/docs/animation.html

Component

```
render: ->
  React.addons.CSSTransitionGroup
    transitionName: 'notification'
  ,
    if @state.notification
      Notification {message: @state.notification}
    else
      []
```

Enter Styles*

```
.notification
  &-enter
    opacity: 0.01
    transition: opacity 0.2s ease-in

    &-active
      opacity: 1

.notification-enter-active
```

Leave Styles*

```
.notification
  &-leave
    opacity: 1
    transition: opacity 0.1s ease-in

    &-active
      opacity: 0.01
```

The children of the transition group are defined conditionally. For example, if we have a notification, we render the notification component, otherwise we must return an empty array (not sure why, but this is required by React). The cool thing about the transition group component is that right when a child is added, it receives the .notification-enter CSS class which we can use to define the initial state of the fade in animation. In this case, that'd be opacity of 0.01 which makes the component barely visible and then we also define the transition for opacity, which would be a 0.2s ease in animation.

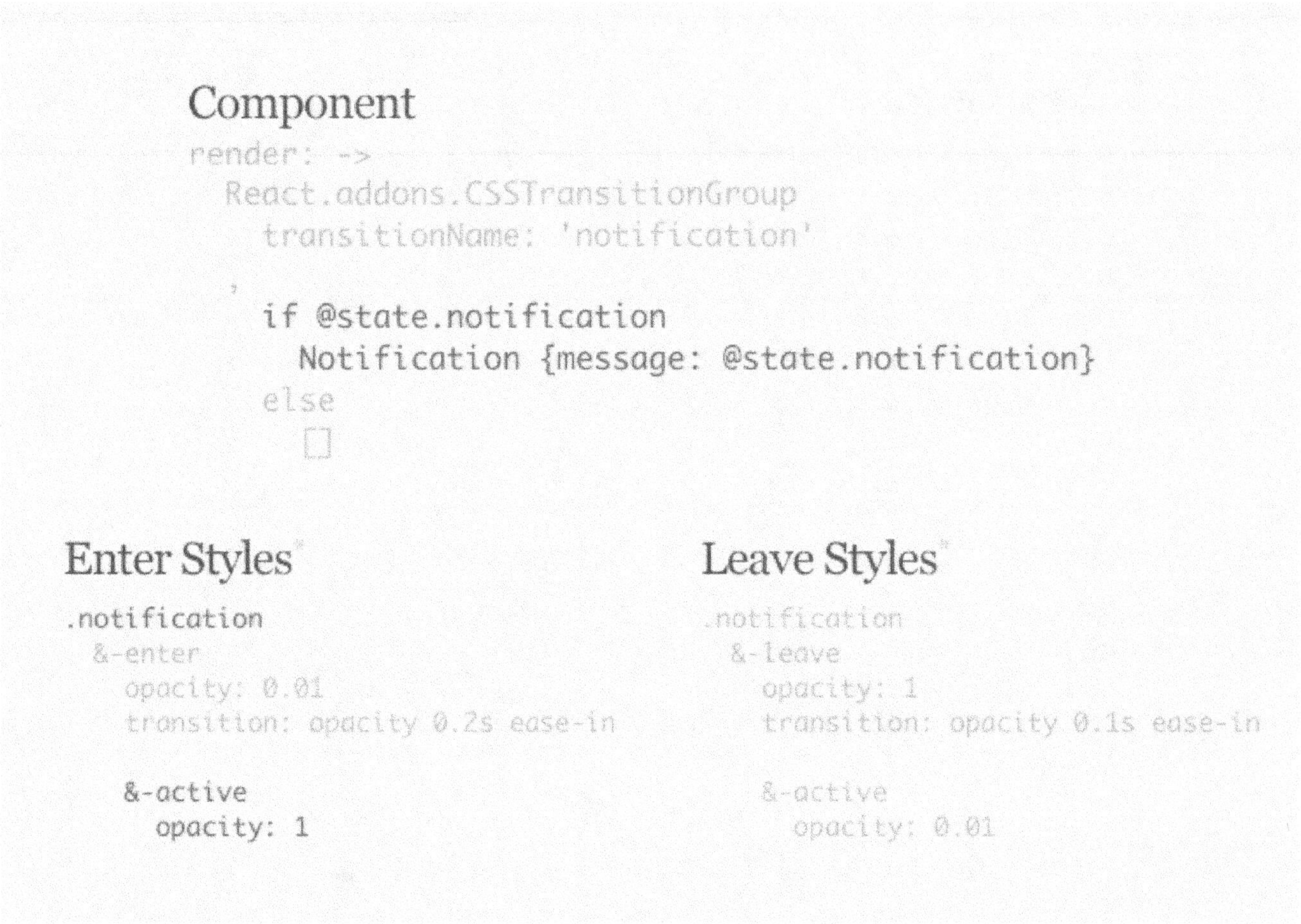

Component

```
render: ->
  React.addons.CSSTransitionGroup
    transitionName: 'notification'
  ,
    if @state.notification
      Notification {message: @state.notification}
    else
      []
```

Enter Styles

```
.notification
  &-enter
    opacity: 0.01
    transition: opacity 0.2s ease-in

    &-active
      opacity: 1
```

Leave Styles

```
.notification
  &-leave
    opacity: 1
    transition: opacity 0.1s ease-in

    &-active
      opacity: 0.01
```

A tick later, React adds the .notification-enter-active CSS class which defines the final state of our animation, in this case making the notification component fully opaque.

Component

```
render: ->
  React.addons.CSSTransitionGroup
    transitionName: 'notification'
  ,
    if @state.notification
      Notification {message: @state.notification}
    else
      []
```

Enter Styles*

```
.notification
  &-enter
    opacity: 0.01
    transition: opacity 0.2s ease-in

    &-active
      opacity: 1
```

Leave Styles*

```
.notification
  &-leave
    opacity: 1
    transition: opacity 0.1s ease-in

    &-active
      opacity: 0.01
```

The opposite happens for the leave animation. Before removing the child from the DOM, React adds the .notification-leave CSS class which defines the initial state of the animation, in this case full opacity and a quicker 0.1s ease in transition.

Component

```
render: ->
  React.addons.CSSTransitionGroup
    transitionName: 'notification'
  ,
    if @state.notification
      Notification {message: @state.notification}
    else
      []
```

Enter Styles

```
.notification
  &-enter
    opacity: 0.01
    transition: opacity 0.2s ease-in

    &-active
      opacity: 1
```

Leave Styles

```
.notification
  &-leave
    opacity: 1
    transition: opacity 0.1s ease-in

    &-active
      opacity: 0.01
```

Again, in the next tick, React adds the .notification-leave-active CSS class which defines the final state of the animation. In this case making the notification component barely visible again before it's finally removed from the DOM.

CHAPTER EIGHT

Why am I excited about React?

* Simple: React is really easy to understand. You tell it what your app looks like at any given point in time and it will make sure your UI automatically reflects that.

* Declarative: React is declarative: You express what your app should look like and not how it is rendered.

* Composable: React is composable: Every component is encapsulated, managing its own behavior and state. Components can be expressed as simple CommonJS modules that can be composed into bigger components while allowing you to test and reason about them independently.

* encourages good practices: By default, React encourages good practices: It encourages you to build small, easy to understand components by making it very simple to do so. It encourages you be very explicit about which way data flows. It encourages you to treat state very deliberately, e.g. how much state do I need and where does it belong? It forces you treat your properties from your parent as immutable. It makes it easy to validate your inputs (properties).

CoffeeScript Streamline.js React.js

Node.js Neo4j

For Questions

You can reach me at Instagram: @sandy41bisht.

www.ingramcontent.com/pod-product-compliance
Lightning Source LLC
Chambersburg PA
CBHW081158130726
47996CB00009B/3167

9798888492857